# Beata Beatrix

## A Play

### Gillian Plowman

A Samuel French Acting Edition

SAMUEL FRENCH

FOUNDED 1830

SAMUELFRENCH-LONDON.CO.UK
SAMUELFRENCH.COM

### FOR AMATEUR PRODUCTION ENQUIRIES

### UNITED KINGDOM AND WORLD
### EXCLUDING NORTH AMERICA
plays@SamuelFrench-London.co.uk
020 7255 4302/01

Each title is subject to availability from Samuel French,

depending upon country of performance.

# Beata Beatrix

First performed by The Flat Four Players with the following cast:

| | |
|---|---|
| **Jon** | David Flint |
| **Beatrice** | Gillian Plowman |
| **Guide** | Jenny Armstrong |
| **Warden** | Ian Armstrong |
| **1st American Tourist** | Robert Iles |
| **2nd American Tourist** | Iris Bartle |
| **Nice Woman** | Frances Iles |

To celebrate ten years

# CHARACTERS

**Beatrice**
**Jon**
**First American Tourist**
**Second American Tourist**
**Nice Woman**
**Guide**
**Attendant**


The action of the play takes place in an art gallery

Time: the present

Other plays by Gillian Plowman, published
by Samuel French Ltd:

Cecily
David's Birthday
The Janna Years
A Kind of Vesuvius
Me and My Friend
Two Summers

# BEATA BEATRIX

*The Pre-Raphaelite room in an art gallery. On the back wall, coloured deep red, are paintings in fine frames. We cannot see any detail; we only have the impression of classical beauty*

*An attendant is sitting silently* UL *at the entrance to the room. Jon is sitting on a bench* C, *staring at a painting on the fourth wall. He is business-suited with white shirt and tie*

*A small group of people enter carrying their art gallery stools, Beatrice among them. They sit and listen to the Guide*

**Guide**  The Pre-Raphaelites wanted to paint contemporary subjects and one of those they found the most interesting was that of the fallen woman. As you know, many women in Victorian times turned to prostitution as the only alternative to starvation. Gentlemen of the day often felt it their duty to "save" these women, although one might question their motives, setting them up in rooms of their own. Hunt's model for this kept woman was Annie Miller, herself a woman of "easy virtue", whom he planned to marry once she was "improved".

*Jon is crying soundlessly and without movement. At some point during the following, Beatrice notices him*

She proved unimprovable. Indeed, had affairs with others of the Pre-Raphaelites, notably Rossetti. Notice the symbolism.

Tremendous detail. This is what the Victorians looked for. A painting told a story. We have films, television… They went to art galleries. Here, a bird is mauled by a cat underneath the table, tangled embroidery silks have fallen to the floor, next to a single glove dropped at her feet—all pointing to the morals of the kept woman who leaps from her lover's lap, flooded with guilt and determining to follow a life of virtue… The half-naked woman trapped under the bell jar holding time in her hands… The score to Tennyson's *Tears, Idle Tears* lying abandoned on the carpet.

**First American Tourist** The score to *Tears, Idle Tears*? I didn't know Tennyson wrote musicals. He was a lord, I know that.

**Second American Tourist** Andrew Lloyd-Webber writes musicals. The Queen has knighted him as well.

**First American Tourist** A knight is not as high as a lord.

**Second American Tourist** It's on the way, though.


*The group moves on and exits right*


*Beatrice does not follow. She stands looking at the painting for a long time. She turns as she hears a low sob from Jon. She hesitates, then moves to look at both him and the painting that he is staring at (Rossetti's Beata Beatrix, for our information). She hesitates, then sits on the same bench, not too close to him*


**Beatrice** Can I help?


*He does not reply. She holds a tissue out to him. He does not take it. There is no-one else there but the attendant. She decides against summoning the attendant. She goes back to the other picture, hesitates, picks up her stool and returns to place it near to Jon*


Please. Dry your eyes.

*She puts the tissue into his hands. It stays there*

>    Please.
**Jon**  Oh dear.
**Beatrice**  Yes. Oh dear.
**Jon**  I'm sorry.
**Beatrice**  Can I—get someone? (*She looks over to the attendant*)
**Jon**  I can't bear it.
**Beatrice**  No.
**Jon**  Can you?

*Pause. Beatrice wonders whether to go. She makes a move, then changes her mind*

**Beatrice**  What?
**Jon**  Her eyes—closed. She is so beautiful. She'll never open them again. She'll never see me. She's dead. Everybody in this room is alive. You're alive. She's dead. (*He cries*)

*Pause*

**Beatrice**  In the paintings, although they're alive—they're all dead now, aren't they? (*She pauses*) The Mona Lisa isn't still alive, except that—she'll be alive for ever.

*He turns to look at her*

>    Your nose.

*She hands him another tissue*

**Jon**  Yes.

*Beatrice looks at the painting with him*

**Beatrice**  I'm not helping.
**Jon**  No.
**Beatrice**  Are you…? I'm not sure what…?

*Pause*

**Jon**  Beatrice.
**Beatrice**  (*surprised*) Yes?
**Jon**  The ideal love of Dante. Rossetti's Beatrice was Elizabeth
   Siddal. His ideal love.
**Beatrice**  Oh. Yes. Beata Beatrix.

*Long pause*

**Jon**  That's Lizzie Siddal.

*Pause*

**Beatrice**  Yes, I know.
**Jon**  And I can't… (*His tears flow once more*)
**Beatrice**  You're crying for Lizzie Siddal?
**Jon**  (*interrupting*) Beatrice.
**Beatrice**  I keep thinking you're…
**Jon**  (*interrupting*) My ideal love.

*Pause. She looks at him*

**Beatrice**  Your ideal l——
**Jon**  (*interrupting*) I walked past her the first time—with someone… I… There are so many… I walked past her. She called
   me back. I had to turn back. I had to—and I did—and when I
   went ba——

*Pause*

**Beatrice** Maybe some fresh a——
**Jon** (*interrupting*) I should never have left her. I left her alone,
   you see, I went... I wanted to go—and she was alone. And
   that's why...

*Pause*

**Beatrice** You're very upset.
**Jon** I have to be with her now.
**Beatrice** Who?

*Jon nods at the painting*

*Pause*

But—it doesn't... It's obviously not doing you any good...
**Jon** Being here...
**Beatrice** Being here——
**Jon** (*interrupting*) I had to have a part of me... Do you see—that
   was for me. But I—she didn't understand—and I... I just
   walked past.

*Pause*

She did understand.

*Pause*

**Beatrice** Well, I——
**Jon** (*interrupting*) But never after that. I never walk past now.
   But she doesn't see.
**Beatrice** No.
**Jon** It's too late.
**Beatrice** Yes.

**Jon**  All the time, I'm here. And she doesn't see.

*Long pause. She gets up*

And that's what happens. You walk out on people, and they die.

*She sits again*

*Pause*

**Beatrice**  I'm afraid I don't understand.
**Jon**  I'm sorry.
**Beatrice**  No, I am.
**Jon**  I should be at work, you know.
**Beatrice**  Should you?
**Jon**  Yes.
**Beatrice**  But it's warm and dry here and you don't have to do anything.

*He looks at her in amazement*

**Jon**  You think I have nothing better to do? Well, you're right. I have nothing better to do. I don't know why you said that.

*Pause*

**Beatrice**  I don't know why I said that. I'm sorry.
**Jon**  No, I am. You shouldn't worry about me.
**Beatrice**  No, I shouldn't. I worry about people.
**Jon**  You shouldn't.
**Beatrice**  I shouldn't. I know. (*She pauses*) I do, though.
**Jon**  You shouldn't.
**Beatrice**  Did… Did someone die?

**Jon** (*whispering*) Yes. She did.

*Pause*

**Beatrice** She...
**Jon** His wife.
**Beatrice** Him?

*He stares at the picture*

Rossetti?
**Jon** Yes. His wife. She died for him. She was so beautiful... He
   painted her—he drew her—she sat for hours, so quiet and
   still...
**Beatrice** She drew him too.
**Jon** You know that?
**Beatrice** He taught her to paint. She was known in her own right
   as a pa——
**Jon** Tell me.
**Beatrice** She was ill for many years.
**Jon** Yes, yes, yes, I know...
**Beatrice** But always drawing and painting. She didn't want to be
   just—a model... People looked down on... And somehow
   they didn't get married, which was the greatest desire of
   Victorian women—their only security.
**Jon** Are you married?
**Beatrice** No. I'm not a Victorian woman.
**Jon** No. And...
**Beatrice** And her work was.
**Jon** He did marry her.
**Beatrice** Yes, he did. In the end. And he was very proud of her
   work.
**Jon** So...

**Beatrice** But she was still ill. She was prescribed laudanum for her pain. She took an overdose. It may—they say—it may have been an accident.

**Jon** I want to save her.

*Pause*

**Beatrice** I don't know how you can do that.
**Jon** No. Don't you see? I can't save her.
**Beatrice** She died in eighteen sixty-two.

*He gets up and moves closer to the painting*

**Jon** He painted that after she was dead. That is her ecstasy; that very point between life and death. Her closed eyes forever shut to me, but gazing upon her new life in heaven. Do you know that they opened her grave two years later because Rossetti wanted his poems back that he had buried with her, and she was just as beautiful as ever, and her—her hair had continued to grow and it was all around her coffin.
**Beatrice** That can't be true, can it?
**Jon** She devoted herself to him and he betrayed her. He was unfaithful—he slept with other women. (*He points to the picture the Guide previously explained*) How could he do that? You understand? You see? His Beatrice.

*Pause*

**Beatrice** I think you should go back to work.
**Jon** I'm seeing my solicitor. I should go back. What do you mean—I should go back to work?
**Beatrice** (*together*) What about?
**Jon** My will. Things aren't getting done at work.

*Pause*

**Beatrice**  You should go back, then. If they can't manage.
**Jon**  They can. My assistant. It's my own business… Exports—
  I've got to meet a man about sending jam to the States. He calls
  it preserves. They call it jelly. I don't know where I am.
**Beatrice**  You're not on your own, though?
**Jon**  Living alone, on my own… I am.
**Beatrice**  At your work.
**Jon**  My assistant…

*Pause. He slumps*

**Beatrice**  She'll manage.
**Jon**  Why do you assume my assistant's a she?
**Beatrice**  Assistants always are. The ones who manage.
**Jon**  Mine's a he so I ought to get back, then.

*Pause*

**Beatrice**  Yes.
**Jon**  But I can't.
**Beatrice**  You can't?
**Jon**  Go. Leave.
**Beatrice**  Shall I come with you?
**Jon**  I'm going to my solicitor.
**Beatrice**  Well, I could come.
**Jon**  Why would you do that?

*Pause*

**Beatrice**  I could be a witness. (*She pauses*) I've got—well, I've
  got the time.

**Jon** Then you'd perjure yourself. You have to witness my being in sound mind, don't you? How could you do that? If I make a will, I have to be in sound mind.

**Beatrice** Don't you think you are?

**Jon** How would I know? But more to the point, how would you know?

**Beatrice** How do you know I am?

**Jon** In sound mind?

**Beatrice** Yes.

**Jon** I think you're not. Why would you—you wouldn't be talking to me... I mean, spending this time with me... You're very kind.

**Beatrice** Don't. I'm not.

**Jon** I didn't mean that being kind was not being in sound mind.

*Beatrice smiles*

I'd rather be on my own, though.

**Beatrice** Oh.

*She gets up*

**Jon** I'm going to commit suicide, you see.

*The Guide and the crowd come back and arrange their stools in front of Jon and Beatrice*

*Everybody sits. Beatrice sits again. They look at the painting*

**Guide** Beata Beatrix by Dante Gabriel Rossetti. Although engaged to Elizabeth Siddal for some ten years, Rossetti only married her two years before her death—some say when he knew she was dying. A year after she died, he began this memorial painting to her. In a letter, he explained, "It is not at all intended to represent Death—but to render it under the resemblance of a trance, in which Beatrice, seated at the balcony overlooking the city is suddenly rapt from earth to heaven." Here are the symbols again… The passion of Beatrice takes place against the form of the cross. Her body is the upright and on either side stand the figures of Love and Dante. The bird, a messenger of death, drops the poppy between the hands of Beatrice…

*Jon stands up. Beatrice stands up*

**Beatrice** I'm awfully sorry. I've just dropped my pearl ear-ring.
**Guide** Oh.

*A Nice Woman looks for the ear-ring. Jon comes forward and speaks to the crowd as though he is the artist, Rossetti*

**Jon** I left her alone, you see. There was never anyone else in her life—she devoted all those years to me. And I loved her. I truly loved her. And I wanted her, as a man wants a woman… Because I loved her. But she was ill, and her life became slower than mine—half of mine. And she wanted to be alone. To work. I… I worked, yes. Yes, I worked, but my life was in two parts. The part that was her life, and the part that was—apart from her. And, God forgive me, I found myself—enjoying that part that was apart from her. I went back—always, I went back, and she would be well, and happy, and busy and full of love, lighting my love, and I renounced that life that was apart from her. Until the next time. And the next time, when I was with another, she died…

*The Guide is unsure what to do*

**Beatrice** You shouldn't blame yourself, Rossetti. Death is an end to suffering, you know. An end to pain. I was looking forward to it.

**Jon** I was with another.

**Beatrice** I know. I know that. I forgive you. Forgive me for not being—all—everything to you. I so wanted to be. But God made you bigger than me. He made you—great. And you made me great. You made me immortal. And I'll be here. I'll wait for you. Just don't come too soon, because… There's lots more for you to do…

**Jon** But I can't—without you… I can't do it.

**Beatrice** "They lose the joy of meeting who never part…"

**Jon** But—to part forever is no joy.

**Beatrice** Not forever, Rossetti. You falter, you fail, and then you rise again. To greater heights. Because you fell. Don't stop because of me. Go on because I stopped.

*Pause*

*The group applaud*

**Guide** The spirit of art transcends mortality.

**First American Tourist** They ought to do that in the galleries back home.

**Nice Woman** I've found your ear-ring.

**Beatrice** Thank you.

*The group get up to exit*

**Second American Tourist** It makes these paintings seem real pertinent, don't it?

*The group go off* L

*Jon and Beatrice are left standing*

**Jon**  It was lucky she found your ear-ring.
**Beatrice**  I don't know how she did that. I've got three now.


*He smiles. She smiles*

You look a little bit like my father when you smile. It was very
rare with him as well.
**Jon**  Was it?
**Beatrice**  But what always made him smile was summer rain
on his roses. Gentle, soft summer rain. He would… Before
the rain had even finished, he would walk all round his
roses, pushing his nose into the wet petals and sniffing very
loudly——
**Jon**  You're like the summer rain.
**Beatrice**  And his carpet slippers would be soaking——
**Jon**  Gentle and soft…
**Beatrice**  And wet!
**Jon**  Wet?
**Beatrice**  Oh, God, I'm wet. I hate people looking at me. I
couldn't be a painting.
**Jon**  But you stood—then—in front of those people.
**Beatrice**  I… So did you. You got something to say, Rossetti, you
say it.
**Jon**  That was nice. You calling me Rossetti.
**Beatrice**  So say it.


*Pause*

**Jon**  If I could paint, I would paint you.
**Beatrice**  Not that.
**Jon**  Yes. That's what I want to say.

**Beatrice**  How often has that been said?

*Pause*

Painters paint young women, wouldn't you say? (*She looks around at the paintings*) Wouldn't you say?

*He moves around some of them*

Or fat duchesses.

*He turns to her*

In the next room.
**Jon**  I would paint you.
**Beatrice**  Because...
**Jon**  Because—your eyes contain the love of mankind.
**Beatrice**  Oh no, they don't. Oh no, they don't. Just because... Just because you're feeling really down...
**Jon**  I'm going to kill myself...
**Beatrice**  Just because you're going to kill yourself, which I didn't know or I wouldn't have stopped at all—I just thought you were feeling ill or something and I get terrible hay fever and feel really bad and nobody ever says, "Would you like a glass of water?" or "Some fresh air would do you good," which it very rarely does when you've got hay fever, so I thought I would just stop, and now you think I'm some sort of...
**Jon**  Saint. Yes.
**Beatrice**  No. I'm an awful person. I... I...
**Jon**  What?
**Beatrice**  Just because I happened to come along at this particular moment in your life—you want to paint me. Oh, for heaven's sake! I wish I hadn't.

**Jon**  Do you?

**Beatrice**  I'm always in the wrong place at the wrong time.
   Even… I mean—always.

**Jon**  You're wrong.

**Beatrice**  My parents thought I was a miracle.

**Jon**  They were r——

**Beatrice**  No! Everybody thought… They were fifty when I was
   born. Waited all their lives for me. They had a shop, and when
   I left school I worked in the shop, too. Just—a corner shop. I
   wanted to travel, but they were old. And they got older. And I
   stayed home.

*Pause*

   Hey, Rossetti, you want a miserable time? I can give you a
   miserable time.

**Jon**  That doesn't make you an awful person.

**Beatrice**  It does. Because I hated them. I didn't. I loved them—
   but why wasn't I born when they were young so that I could
   have been young? So that I could have… I could have… There
   was this pile of garden rubbish and… The garden was a mess—
   I had to do it, and I'd made them both lunch and they were
   asleep, so I had a bonfire, and I was full of hate and self-pity
   because I wanted to be anywhere else but there, and I shovelled
   the pile on to the bonfire, and there was this screaming sound.

*Pause*

   I'd shovelled a nest of baby creatures—I couldn't even see
   what they were—on to the fire. I couldn't see them through my
   tears of self-pity. And they perished. And I can't get that out of
   my head. The sight of those little creatures curling up in
   agony… I did that.

**Jon**  By mistake.
**Beatrice**  It happened.

*Pause*

My parents have gone now, and I've sold the corner shop, and
the rooms behind where I lived all my life, and that garden, and
I've got a flat. And I haven't the courage to travel. As I say,
I'm wet.

*Pause*

And I can't get that out of my mind.
**Jon**  Did you ever tell anybody before?
**Beatrice**  No.
**Jon**  Thank you, then.
**Beatrice**  I wouldn't have told you; only, you're a stranger and
you're going to commit suicide anyway. Rossetti didn't. Why
are you?
**Jon**  You talk about it as though I'm not.
**Beatrice**  You're not!
**Jon**  I am!
**Beatrice**  Why should you?
**Jon**  I don't want to live any more.
**Beatrice**  What have you done that is so bad you can't live
with it?
**Jon**  I've told you.
**Beatrice**  What?
**Jon**  You know why.
**Beatrice**  No, I don't.
**Jon**  I was with another.

*Pause*

**Beatrice** Tell me.

**Jon** Thank you very much for everything. I've really got to see
my solicitor now.

**Beatrice** Does he know?

**Jon** What?

**Beatrice** About the suicide? It might invalidate the will.

**Jon** That's insurance.

**Beatrice** I think you ought to tell him.

**Jon** Mind your own business.

**Beatrice** Are you going to disappear? Someone ought to know.
How are you going to do it? I mean, are you going to be found?

**Jon** I expect so.

**Beatrice** And who's going to find you?

**Jon** Somebody.

**Beatrice** Somebody? Like Rossetti when he came home and
found Lizzie? Found the note pinned to her dress which "left
such a scar on his heart as would never be healed". Who?

**Jon** I don't know.

**Beatrice** Your wife? Your children?

*Pause*

**Jon** No.

**Beatrice** Are your friends going to find you?

**Jon** Once—Evie was pregnant and we both agreed—to termi-
nate the pregnancy. Until later. It wasn't convenient. When she
got leukaemia, Evie thought—it was her punishment. She said
"Yours will come as well, Jon". It did. I lost her.

**Beatrice** Evie?

**Jon** My wife.

**Beatrice** She...

**Jon** Died.

**Beatrice** Of leukaemia?

**Jon** Yes.
**Beatrice** I'm so sorry.
**Jon** She was in the hospital a long time. I went to bed with somebody else. The night she died... I didn't know—they didn't know—I was in bed with somebody else. My punishment.
**Beatrice** How long...? When did she die?
**Jon** Yesterday. It seems. But... Two years now. I never wrote her poems... She had no poems to take with her. I wanted to write her poems but—I can't. (*He pauses*) And... She didn't have any hair. The chemotherapy, you see. Do you see?
**Beatrice** Yes.
**Jon** Do you think it grew again?

*Beatrice doesn't know how to reply*

Of course, I know it didn't.
**Beatrice** No.
**Jon** She understood.
**Beatrice** What?
**Jon** Me. She understood me.
**Beatrice** She loved you.
**Jon** And I was in bed with somebody else.
**Beatrice** What happened to the—somebody else?
**Jon** Went back to Canada. Exports, you know.
**Beatrice** It's a funny business, exports.
**Jon** Yes.
**Beatrice** Poor Jon.

*She takes his hand. He lets her*

In the shop, you know, I used to wonder about exports.
**Jon** Did you.
**Beatrice** There were so many things from so many places: butter

from New Zealand, bacon from Denmark, honey from Mexico. And gorgonzola. What did we send to them, I wondered. And why is this stuff flitting about the world? We have bees. And pigs and milk. We can do honey and bacon and butter.

**Jon**  We can't do gorgonzola.

**Beatrice**  No, but do the Italians eat mature farmhouse cheddar? Well, you would know. Do we export that?

**Jon**  We send cheese to Canada.

**Beatrice**  Ah. So your friend was in cheese?

**Jon**  What friend?

**Beatrice**  The one you were in bed with.

**Jon**  She wasn't in cheese. Don't talk about her.

**Beatrice**  Don't talk about her! The woman who's ruined my life.

**Jon**  What?

**Beatrice**  What's her name?

**Jon**  I don't know.

**Beatrice**  You went to bed with her.

**Jon**  I've forgotten. How has she ruined your life?

**Beatrice**  You're going to jump off a bridge for her.

**Jon**  I'm not going to jump off a bridge.

**Beatrice**  Throw yourself under a train for her.

**Jon**  I'm not. Not for her.

**Beatrice**  What are you going to do then? I've got to live with it, whatever it is. That's what she's done to me.

**Jon**  You've got to live with it. Leave me alone. You don't have to do anything.

**Beatrice**  You mean walk out of here, get some sausages for tea and have you on my conscience? You should be on her conscience, not mine. I can't… I can't… I can't live with those creatures on the bonfire… Jon… She's got to live with this, not me.

**Jon**  It's nothing to do with her. She didn't know about Evie. She didn't do it on purpose.

**Beatrice**  I didn't meet you on purpose. Did I? Did I? And now

I'm lumbered with a tragedy. We've got to export this whole thing to Canada. To… To who? Tell me.

**Jon** Carla. I think her name was Carla. But I don't know where… We never actually did any business.

**Beatrice** Only funny business. Eh? Eh? Carla who?

**Jon** I don't know.

**Beatrice** You know!

**Jon** Carla Mulholland.

**Beatrice** And whereabouts in Canada did she come from?

**Jon** Toronto.

**Beatrice** And what did she look like?

**Jon** Tall. Dark. Her eyes were blue and… I told her I loved her. That's what I did. That's what I did.

**Beatrice** And did you?

**Jon** When I was holding her—yes.

**Beatrice** And she left you?

**Jon** Yes.

**Beatrice** I shall go to Toronto. Yes. I'll find Carla Mulholland, and I'll—give her your suicide. I'm not having it!

**Jon** Oh, so at last you're going to go travelling, are you? Couldn't manage it before—too exciting, too adventurous, didn't know how to start? Now you're using me as an excuse, going to look up my friends.

**Beatrice** I can't see that she's any friend of yours!

**Jon** Because you haven't got the guts to go off on your own.

**Beatrice** And you didn't have the guts to sleep on your own!

**Jon** I imagine you've slept on your own most of your life.

*Pause*

**Beatrice** Goodbye, Rossetti.

**Jon** Jon Williams.

**Beatrice** Goodbye.

**Jon**  I'm sorry.

*She turns to go. He restrains her*

Please. I'm sorry.
**Beatrice**  Don't be. Life's too short. Excuse me.
**Jon**  No… I… Listen, please, I don't know your name…
**Beatrice**  Excuse me.
**Jon**  You've been… I don't want you to go just like that.
**Beatrice**  I don't care what you want. Want, want, want. I've got
   a lot of things to do, please let go of my arm, let go of me, I want
   to go!

*The attendant walks past as he sees them struggle and they stand
still as he goes and sits at the other end of the room, in the
shadows. Jon and Beatrice stand and look at each other*

No. I have never slept with a man. I have never been anybody's
ideal love. Not like Lizzie Siddal. Not like your Evie. Not even
like Carla Mulholland. (*She sits on the seat and looks at Beata
Beatrix*) And you know, the funny thing is, my name really is
Beatrice.
**Jon**  Beatrice. Is it?
**Beatrice**  Yes.
**Jon**  Beatrice.
**Beatrice**  I come in here too, you know. I come in here and long
   for a life. I look at her and inside me I'm crying, not because
   she's dead but because I've never lived.

*Jon hands her a tissue*

And you. You've known it all. Love, hate, betrayal, guilt.
Ecstasy. And (*she blows hard*) you're going to ditch the lot.
Your Evie died for nothing, then? Hey, Rossetti, you're a fool.

**Jon**  I'm not doing it. If you're going to make such a fuss
    about it...
**Beatrice**  Me! I was just on a guided tour.
**Jon**  I don't know why, you seem to know it all...
**Beatrice**  My tenth guided tour.
**Jon**  Tenth?
**Beatrice**  Ask me why.
**Jon**  Why, Beatrice?
**Beatrice**  Oh, that's nice.
**Jon**  Why?
**Beatrice**  Because... I keep hoping I'll meet somebody.

*They get up and start walking towards the exit*

**Jon**  Quite a good way of meeting people, I should think.
**Beatrice**  Yes. Only I'm a bit shy, so I've never quite managed
    to start off a conversation.
**Jon**  Talk about the paintings, I would say. I mean, that's what
    everybody's here for, isn't it? That's the common factor.

*They start to go*

**Beatrice**  This is the room with the fat duchesses.
**Jon**  Are you happy with fat duchesses, or would you like a
    coffee?

*Music starts*

**Beatrice**  That's a good idea.

CURTAIN

# FURNITURE AND PROPERTY LIST

*On stage:*    Paintings in fine frames
Bench
2 **Attendant**'s stools

*Off stage:*    Art gallery stools (**Guided Tour Group**)

*Personal:*    **Beatrice:** tissues
**Nice Woman:** ear-ring
**Jon:** tissue

# LIGHTING PLOT

Property fittings required: nil
Interior. The same scene throughout

*To open:*  Overall general lighting

*No cues*

# EFFECTS PLOT

*Cue* 1  **Jon**: "…would you like a coffee?"  (Page 22)
    *Music*